THE EFFECTS OF THE JUVENILE JUSTICE SYSTEM ON SELF-CONCEPT

DENNIS C. BLISS

San Francisco, California
1977

Published by

R & E RESEARCH ASSOCIATES, INC.
4843 Mission Street
San Francisco, California 94112

Publishers
Robert D. Reed and Adam S. Eterovich

Library of Congress Card Catalog Number

76-55965

I.S.B.N.
0-88247-433-2

ACKNOWLEDGEMENT

I would like to express my appreciation to Dr. William Faulkner, Dr. Giri Raj Gupta, and especially to Dr. Steven Cox. Dr. Cox initially stimulated my interest in deviance and offered his utmost in assistance and encouragement. Also, I would like to thank Mr. James Grundel, Director of Court Services for Knox County, Mr. Randall Storm, superintendent of the detention facility, and the activities director, Mr. John Reed. And last but not least, my wife, Glenda, who, aside from her companionship and inspiration, typed the manuscript with great patience and skill.

TABLE OF CONTENTS

LIST OF TABLES

CHAPTER I

INTRODUCTION

Juvenile delinquency is a major social problem in the United States today. In 1967 youths under eighteen years of age constituted twenty-four percent of the total 5.5 million persons arrested.[1] "They account for almost three-fourths of all arrests for burglary, larceny, and auto theft."[2] These figures do not include those youths who were not apprehended by the police. It is apparent that there is a trend toward an increase in delinquency in our society. The California Youth Authority conducted a study to provide some guidelines for understanding the "average" juvenile delinquent. It was found that the average offender had delinquent contacts prior to admission to the Youth Authority. Eighty-nine percent had two or more prior delinquent contacts, and only three percent had none.[3] The delinquent behavior pattern depicted by the California Youth Authority is very similar to the pattern revealed by the juvenile court statistics of the entire nation.

A primary objective of the juvenile court is to prevent the juvenile from being labeled a criminal by society which may lead him to perceive himself as criminal.[4] But, research on delinquency leads one to believe that the juvenile courts have been unsuccessful in attempting to prevent the individual from obtaining a "spoiled" identity.

The purpose of this study is to determine if a significant difference in self-concept exists among institutionalized delinquents, delinquents on probation, and a control group of non-delinquents in a small midwestern community. If the labeling perspective to be discussed below is correct, institutionalized delinquents should have the most negative self-concepts, followed by delinquents on probation, and non-delinquents should have more positive self-concepts. Self-concept will be measured by Kuhn and McPartland's Twenty Statements Test, a

1

modified version of William Fitt's Tennessee Self Concept Test, and by interview. First we will turn to a literature review for discussion of the symbolic inter-actionist school, its relationship to the labeling approach, and a review of the previous research in this area.

CHAPTER II

LITERATURE REVIEW

Symbolic Interaction

Over the last decade the labeling perspective has gained prominence in
the United States as a major sociological approach to understanding the nature
of deviance. The labeling perspective considers how social actors become
defined and treated as deviant rather than the traditional etiological question
of what makes social actors commit deviant acts. From this perspective, the study
of deviance includes not only the alleged deviant, but also the reactions of
others and especially the reactions of agencies of social control established to
deal with deviance. In other words, the context surrounding the social actor
becomes the primary focus of research.

More than two decades have elapsed since Edwin Lemert formulated some
of the major assumptions of the labeling perspective. Since that time due to
subsequent refinements of the perspective, a substantial body of theoretical and
empirical evidence has been accumulated in support of its main tenets. Writers
often cited as representative of this "societal reactions approach," "labeling
theory," and the interactionist orientation" include Kai T. Erikson, John I.
Kitsuse, Howard S. Becker, Edwin M. Schur, and Harold Garfinkle. The works of
these sociologists will be discussed in depth shortly, but first it is essential
to examine the primary assumptions of the labeling perspective.

A fundamental tenet of the labeling perspective is that deviance is
the product of interaction between an actor and a social audience. This places
deviance in a framework external to (but not detached from) the actor, and subject
to the process of identification and reaction by others. "From this point of view,
defiance is not a quality of an act a person commits, but rather a consequence of
the application by others of rules and sanctions to an 'offender'. The deviant

is one to whom that label has been successfully applied; deviant behavior is behavior that people so label."[5]

Conceptualization of deviance as a "reaction process" on the part of others leads to the recognition that the distinction between conventional and unconventional behavior is very ambiguous. According to the labeling approach, acceptable and unacceptable designations for behavior are relative. There are inherent ambiguities involved in the distinction of whether an act is deviant or non-deviant.

The labeling perspective originates, in part, from an interactionist framework. The interactionist framework is a perspective which emphasizes the collective nature of social action, the dynamics of interaction between self and others, and the importance of seeing reality from the point of view of those engaged in the action. This perspective not only allows for the incorporation of the preceding points into a framework for understanding deviance, but behavior in general.

While the roots of symbolic interactionism extend to the works of many writers (Weber, Simmel, Baldwin, James, etc.) three of these authors are of specific interest for present purposes. They are: George Herbert Mead, Charles Horton Cooley, and W. I. Thomas. Some major contributions of each to the symbolic interactionist perspective (out of which labeling theory largely emerged) are discussed below.

Social psychology, for George Herbert Mead, is the discipline that "studies the activity or behavior of the individual as it lies within the social process. The behavior of the individual can be understood only in terms of the behavior of the whole social group of which he is a member, since his individual acts are involved in larger, social acts which go beyond himself and which implicate the others members of that group."[6] Mead argued that there can be no self

4

apart from society, no consciousness of self and no communication. Society emerges through an ongoing process of communicative social acts and through transactions between persons who are mutually oriented toward each other. When the individual is a social object to himself, he has a self. To be an object to oneself is to be aware of the meaning one's gestures to other participants in the social act. By taking the attitude of the other toward his own gestures, the individual responds implicitly to his own behavior; and he is thus conscious of himself because he is aware of his own behavior as a phase of a more inclusive social act.

According to Mead, to be an object to oneself is not to be merely aware of the physical activity of one's body. Rather it is to be aware of one's behavior as a part of a social process. "The self has the characteristic that it is an object to itself, and that characteristic distinguishes it from other objects and from the body."[7] In short, the individual can look at himself only from the standpoint of another, and the means for doing this is role-taking. Taking the role of the other is equivalent to being aware of the response one's actions will evoke in the other.

The fully mature individual, according to Mead, does not merely take into account the attitudes of other individuals, of "significant others", toward himself and toward one another; he must also "take their attitudes toward the various phases or aspects of the common social activity...in which, as members of an organized society or social group, they are all engaged."[8] Only insofar as he takes the attitudes of the social group to which he belongs toward social activity does he develop a complete self. The mature self arises when a generalized other is internalized so that the community exercises control over the conduct of its individual members. "Mead maintains that the generalized other is the social, cognitive, rational component of the self. It is invoked whenever a person considers what he ought to do, and no person can consider what he ought to do and no one can be conscious of what he is doing without involving the generalized other."[9]

As Mead points out, there are general rules used as guides to moral conduct, but these rules are not recipes stating in detail how one should act. What one ought to do in any particular situation cannot be found in a moral hand-book. Rules of the game and ethical principles serve as general guidelines, but there are an unlimited number of possible ways of performing or carrying out one's social role that fall within the limits of the rules of the game and ethical principles. Mead's concept of the self is thus very important in explaining how a person comes to be termed deviant and how he perceives his deviancy. It is essential, at this point, to define deviance. "'Deviance,' in current American sociology, refers to any behavior or attribute for which an individual is regarded as objectionable in a particular social system. It denotes anything that violates prevailing norms on what makes a person acceptable."[10] There is nothing inherently deviant in any human act; something is deviant only because some people have been successful in labeling it so and, according to Mead, one considers himself a deviant only when he sees himself as such by taking the role of others in his web of interactions.

Like Mead, Charles Horton Cooley argued that a person's self grows out of his interaction with others. "The social origin of his life comes by the pathway of intercourse with other persons."[11] The self is not first individual and then social; it arises dialectically through communication. One's conscious-ness of himself is a reflection of the ideas about himself that he attributes to other minds; thus, there can be no isolated selves. "There is no sense of 'I'... without its correlative sense of you, or he, or they."[12]

Cooley compared the reflected character of the self to a looking glass.

"As we see our face, figure, and dress in the glass, and are interested in them because they are ours, and pleased or otherwise with them according as they do or do not answer to what we should like them to be, so in imagination we perceive in another's mind some thought of our appearance, manners, aims, deeds, character, friends, and so on, and are variously affected by it."[13]

The concept of the looking-glass self is composed of three principle elements: "The imagination of our appearance to the other person, the imagination of his judgment of that appearance, and some sort of self-feeling, such as pride or mortification."[14] The self is developed in the process of interaction with others. Cooley states: "Society is an interweaving and interworking of mental selves. I imagine your mind, and especially what your mind thinks about my mind, and what your mind thinks about what my mind thinks about your mind. I dress my mind before yours and expect that you will dress yours before mine. Whoever cannot or will not perform these feats is not properly in the game."[15]

William I. Thomas asserts, "Preliminary to any self-determined act of behavior there is always a stage of examination and deliberation which we may call 'the definition of the situation.' And actually not only concrete acts are dependent on the definition of the situation, but gradually a whole life-policy and the personality of the individual himself follow from a series of such definitions."[16] The child is born into a world in which all the general types of situations which may arise have already been defined and corresponding rules of conduct developed. He does not have the chance of making decisions and following his wishes without interference. "There is therefore always a rivalry between the spontaneous definitions of the situation made by the member of an organized society and the definitions which his society has provided for him. The individual tends to a hedonistic selection of activity, pleasure first; and society to a utilitarian selection, safety, first."[17] Society desires its members to be laborious, orderly, dependable, sober, etc., and seeks to regulate conflict and competition between its members. "It is in this connection that a moral code arises, which is a set of rules or behavior norms, regulating the expression of the wishes, and which is built up by successive definitions of the situation."[18] Morality is the generally accepted definition of the situation, whether expressed in public opinion and unwritten law, a formal legal code, or in religious mandates and prohibitions.

According to Thomas, the community knows how to scorn persons and actions by using words and phrases such as: "coward", "whore", "traitor", "snob", etc., which are brief and emotional definitions of the situation. Laughter, sneers, shrugs, coldness, etc., are also language defining the situation and felt as unfavorable recognition. Fear is used by the group to produce the desired behavior in its members. Praise is also used but more sparingly. "...The whole body of habits and emotions is so much a community and family product that disapproval or separation is almost unbearable."[19]

Labeling Theory

"At the heart of the labeling approach is an emphasis on process; deviance is viewed not as a static entity but rather as a continuously shaped and reshaped outcome of dynamic processes of social interaction."[20] It is in this general theme of process, concentration on deviant roles, and the development of deviant self-conceptions that one can clearly see the indebtedness of labeling analysis to the theoretical perspective of symbolic interactionism. Mead saw the self as a process rather than a structure. Schemes that seek to explain the self through structure alone ignore the reflexive process that Mead recognized as central to social interaction. "The human being is seen as an active organism in his own right, facing, dealing with, and acting toward the objects he indicates."[21]

Social patterns reflect a continuous process of fitting developing lines of conduct to one another. The actor is viewed as "largely at the mercy of the reaction processes; what they are determines what he is to become."[22]

The relationship between the symbolic interactionist tradition and the labeling approach to the study of deviance is complex. The works of Edwin Lemert are among the more important in pointing out the nature of this relationship. It was he who developed the core concepts of primary and secondary deviance and developed a view of norm-creating and deviance labeling that stressed the lack of normative integration of modern society and the opportunity for many diverse and self-interested organizations to impose special moral and legal standards on behavior. He related deviance to processes of social differentiation and social definition. Lemert stated: "We start with the idea that persons and groups are differentiated in various ways, some of which result in social penalties, rejection, and segregation. These penalties and segregative reactions of society or the community are dynamic factors which increase, decrease, and condition the form which the initial differentiation or deviation takes."[23] Also, he asserted, "The deviant person is one whose roles, status, function, and self-definition are importantly shaped by how much deviation he engaged in, by the degree of its social visibility, by the particular exposure he has to the societal reaction, and by the strength of the societal reaction."[24]

One of the leaders in the "societal reaction" school is Kai T. Erikson. Building upon Durkheim's ideas of the functions of deviance in societies, Erikson develops an approach to deviance which stresses the functions of deviance and deviance definition as central to the maintenance of social boundaries and community identity. People know who and what they are in terms of who and what they condemn. It follows that a continuing group identity requires a continuing condemnation. Erikson defines deviance as "conduct which is generally thought to require the attention of social control agencies -- that is, conduct about which 'something should be done.' Deviance is not a property inherent in certain forms of behavior; it is a property conferred upon these forms by the audiences which directly or indirectly witness them."[25] The critical variable in deviance, then, becomes the audience rather than the actor, since the former determines whether or not the latter will be labeled deviant.

Erikson contends that the process of creating deviants is highly selective. In many cases, one deviant act alone is sufficient to convince society that an individual is now, always has been, and always will be a deviant. As Erikson points out, the audience which defines an actor as deviant often considers many factors which are not directly related to the deviant act: "It is sensitive to the suspect's social class, his past record as an offender, the amount of remorse he manages to convey, and many similar concerns which take hold in the shifting moods of the community."[26] Erikson continues: "Because the range of human behavior is potentially so wide, social groups maintain boundaries in the sense that they try to limit the flow of behavior within their domain so that it circulates within a defined cultural territory. Boundaries, then, are an important point of reference for persons participating in any system."[27] Boundaries may be defined in a variety of ways, but in any case, they serve to indicate an individual's position relative to others in the community. Transactions taking place between deviant persons and agencies of control are boundary maintaining mechanisms. "They mark the outside limits of the area within which the norm has jurisdiction, and in this way assert how much diversity and variability can be contained within the system before it begins to lose its distinctive structure, its cultural integrity."[28]

The community's decision to bring sanctions against an individual is not a simple act of censure. The decision moves the individual out of his

10

normal position in society and transfers him into a distinct deviant role. According to Erikson, ceremonies which accomplish this change of status usually consist of three related phases. They provide a formal confrontation between the deviant suspect and the representatives of his community (the criminal trial or psychiatric case conference); they announce some judgment about the nature of his deviancy (a verdict or diagnosis, for example); and they perform an act of social placement, assigning him to a special role (like that of a prisoner or patient) which redefines his position in society.

An important feature of these ceremonies in our own culture is that they tend to be irreversible. "Most provisional roles conferred by society -- like those of the student or conscripted soldier, for example -- include some kind of terminal ceremony to mark the individual's movement back out of the role once its temporary advantages have been exhausted. But the roles allotted to the deviant seldom make allowance for this type of passage."[29] Nothing happens to cancel out the stigmas imposed upon him by earlier commitment ceremonies.

Robert Merton's "self-fulfilling prophesy"[30] is a good phrase to describe what takes place when the ex-deviant returns to society. The community's reluctance to accept the deviant back reduces whatever chance he might have had for a successful readjustment.

> "If the returning deviant has to face the community's appre-
> hensions often enough, it is understandable that he too may
> begin to wonder whether he has graduated from the deviant
> role -- and respond to the uncertainty by resuming deviant
> activity. In some respects, this may be the only way for
> the individual and his community to agree as to what kind of
> person he really is, for it often happens that the community
> is only able to perceive his 'true colors' when he lapses
> momentarily into some form of deviant performance."[31]

John Kitsuse also focuses on the processes by which persons come to be defined as deviant by others. According to Kitsuse, the forms of behavior per se do not activate the processes of societal reaction which differentiate deviants from non-deviants. He asks: "What are the behaviors which are defined by members of the group, community, or society as deviant, and how do those definitions organize and activate the societal reactions by which persons come to be differentiated and treated as deviants?"[32] Kitsuse states that, "deviance may be conceived as a process by which the members of a group, community, or society 1.) interpret behavior as deviant, 2.) define persons who so behave as a certain kind of deviant, and 3.) accord them the treatment considered appropriate to such deviants."[33]

Kitsuse found that an individual's "normality" may be called into question with reference to two broad categories of evidence. Indirect evidence in the form of rumor was frequently a cause for suspecting an individual to be "different." Information of this type is often accepted without independent verification. This information provides a new perspective for both retrospective and prospective observations and interpretations of the "deviant's" behavior. Direct observation by the subject of an individual's behavior may also be the basis for calling his "normality" into question. Kitsuse indicates that an individual is particularly suspect when he behaves in a manner which deviates from the behaviors-held-in-common among members of the group to which he belongs. Kitsuse further argued that the imputation of deviance is documented by retrospective interpretations of the deviant's behavior, a process by which the subject reinterprets the individual's past behavior in the light of the new information concerning his deviance. "The subjects indicate that they reviewed their past interactions with the individuals in question, searching for subtle cues and nuances of behavior which might give further evidence of the alleged deviance. This retrospective reading generally provided the subjects with just such evidence to support the conclusion that 'this is what was going on all the time.'[34]

Another proponent of the labeling approach, Howard S. Becker, sees deviance as a "Creation of society."[35] "Society," according to Becker, "creates

rules whose infraction constitutes deviance."[36] Deviance does not depend on the

act one commits, but rather it is a consequence of the application by others of

rules to an "offender." "Deviant behavior is behavior that people label as

such."[37] Becker makes the important point that in studying deviants, one may

not assume that they have committed a deviant act or broken some rule, because

the process of labeling may not be infallible; some people may be labeled

deviant who have not broken a rule. Particularly crucial for present purposes

is the fact that one cannot assume that the category of those labeled deviant

will contain all those who have actually broken a rule, because many offenders

may escape apprehension and thus fail to be in the population of deviants one

studies. Studies of juvenile delinquency often fall into this category. "Boys

from middle-class areas do not get as far in the legal process when they are

apprehended as do boys from slum areas. The middle-class boy is less likely,

when picked up by the police, to be taken to the station; less likely when taken

to the station to be booked; and it is extremely unlikely he will be convicted

and sentenced."[38]

To be labeled deviant, one need only commit a single offense, but the

deviant may then be viewed as possessing additional deviant traits. "Treating a

person as though he were generally rather than specifically deviant produces a

self-fulfilling prophecy"[39] or what Becker refers to as a "master status." It

sets in motion several mechanisms which shape the person in the image others have

of him. The deviant is often excluded from participation in conventional groups,

even though the specific consequences of the particular deviant activity might

never have caused the isolation had there not also been the public knowledge and

reaction to it. When the deviant is caught, he is treated in accordance with the

popular diagnosis of why he is that way, and the treatment itself may produce increasing deviance. "The behavior is a consequence of the public reaction to the deviance rather than a consequence of the inherent qualities of the deviant act."[40]

Edwin M. Schur defines deviance in the following terms: "Human behavior is deviant to the extent that it comes to be viewed as involving a personally discreditable departure from a group's normative expectations, and it elicits interpersonal or collective reactions that serve to 'isolate,' 'treat,' 'correct,' or 'punish' individuals engaged in such behavior."[41] He continues: "...It is the degree to which such definitions and responses are elicited, rather than the formal possibility they could be, that determines the 'extent of deviantness.'"[42] A departure from the norm that could be but is not condemned or punished under existing formal rules is less deviant than it would be if negative sanctions were actually applied.

Schur's discussion emphasizes the fact that the deviantness of an act or individual is always relative, changeable, and a matter of degree. The degree depends mainly on the extent to which the behavior is viewed and responded to in certain ways.

In the labeling approach, stereotyping is a central component of the social processes of which deviance is created. Schur asserts that social typing is continuous. Just as the individual constantly types other people, he is constantly being typed by others and also by himself. "Deviants are persons who are typed socially in a very special sort of way. They are assigned to certain categories and each category carries with it a stock interpretative accounting for any persons subsumed under its rubric."[43]

Stereotyping, in direct personal interaction, may significantly influence the expectations of others, causing serious problems of response and "identity management,"[44] for deviators. Definitions of the situation held by those reacting to the deviation, definitions that are often shaped primarily by stereotyped beliefs, can be so overwhelming that the deviating individual may find himself unable to sustain any alternative definition. "Stereotyping can serve at all levels, to instigate or propel mechanisms of the self-fulfilling prophecy, in which the conditions that control measures are aimed at are fostered by those very measures."[45]

The second facet of the labeling process, Schur states, is retrospective interpretation. This involves the mechanisms by which reactors come to view deviators or suspected deviators in a new light. The most obvious examples are found in public "status-degradation ceremonies,"[46] which will be discussed in detail, shortly. An individual perceived one day as "normal," can, as a result of conviction at a trial or even of having been held as a suspect, become a murderer or rapist the next. The ramifications of rereading an individual are basic to the way in which the labeling process creates deviants. Garfinkel states:

> The work of the denunciation effects the recasting of the objective character of the perceived other: The other person becomes in the eyes of his condemners literally a different and new person. It is not that the new attributes are added to the old "nucleus." He is not changed, he is reconstituted. The former identity, at best, receives the accent of mere appearance...the former identity stands as accidental; the new identity is the "basic reality." What he is now is what, "after all," he was all along.[47]

Any communicative work between persons, whereby the public identity of an actor is transformed into something looked on as lower in the local scheme of social types may be termed a status degradation ceremony. Harold Garfinkel discussed this in his article "Conditions of Successful Degradation Ceremonies."[48] The purpose of these ceremonies is to transform the actor into something viewed as being inferior in the local social structure. Degradation makes the perpetrator a scapegoat for the rest of society. He is used as an example to all others like him in the hope that others may be rehabilitated by this example. The deviant must be totally destroyed and replaced, not just overhauled. The degradation must be total (both the behavior and the grounds for his behavior), and it must be public.

If the individual is convicted of a serious crime and labeled as deviant by the generalized other, he may have virtually no alternative but to accept this label. More than likely it will stay with him the rest of his life. His conception of himself as a deviant and an ex-convict will be re-inforced by others wherever he ventures.

It would appear that the implications of labeling one deviant can be very severe. This is a primary reason for the differentiation between the criminal court system and the juvenile court system to which we now turn our attention. The belief is that it is unfair to apply a criminal label to a youthful offender, in most cases, due to his immaturity and the fact that he still has time to reform and become a useful and contributing member of society.

When an adult is arrested for a crime, his punishment is set by local, state, or federal statutes. On the other hand, the juvenile offender, seventeen years and younger in Illinois, usually is not charged with a crime, depending on the nature of the act. Station House Adjustments are common in juvenile offen-ses. Approximately fifty to sixty percent of new offenders are released with-out charge after a consultation with the parents.[49] In those cases where formal action is taken, instead of being charged with a crime as an adult is, a peti-tion is filed against the juvenile, which begins, "In the interests of John Doe, a juvenile..." A preliminary hearing, in which bail is set for the adult, cor-responds to the preliminary conference for the juvenile. At this time, probation officials try to persuade the complainant not to sign a petition against the juvenile if it is his first offense or if there is evidence the juvenile will

16

not attempt such an act again. The grand jury hearing performs an investigating function in the criminal court; at the arraignment the adult enters a plea; is found guilty or not guilty in criminal court. For the juvenile an adjudicatory hearing is held to determine if the youth is to be termed delinquent. If not, all proceedings are halted. The youth has the same rights as the adult in this case. If he is found delinquent, a social background investigation is held. These findings are considered when the dispositional hearing is held. At this time the judge determines the future of the delinquent. He may be placed on probation in custody of his parents or foster parents, placed with foster parents, disposed of in a detention facility, sent to the Department of Mental Health for care, or, as a last resort, placed in the Juvenile Branch of the State Department of Corrections.

The Juvenile Court is supposed to be confidential and records are theoretically inaccessable except to officials and legitimate researchers. The hearing is closed to the public. Only family, others involved in the case, researchers, and the press are admitted. The press may give an account of the case, but no names may be used except in special instances. No minor under sixteen may be confined in jail as a result of police action, rather he may be sent to a detention facility to await his hearing. Minors between sixteen and seventeen may not be confined in the same facilities as adult prisoners. Juvenile records must be kept separate from adult records and cannot be viewed without a court order. When the juvenile reaches twenty-one and has not been in any further trouble, his juvenile records are destroyed.

From the foregoing discussion, then, it is clear that one purpose of the juvenile court is to prevent the juvenile from being labeled a criminal by the generalized other, which may lead him to perceive himself as criminal. The extent to which it is successful in this endeavor is an important empirical question.

Previous Research

The labeling approach leads one to believe that being publicly identi-
fied as deviant results in a "spoiled" public identity. It contends that being
labeled deviant results in a degree of social liability, such as exclusion from
participation in certain conventional groups or activities, which would not occur
if the deviance were not made a matter of public knowledge. It further suggests
that the social liability incurred by being labeled deviant has the ultimate
effect of reinforcing the deviance, because public assignment to a deviant
status negatively affects the deviant's interpersonal relationships with others
(e.g., family, peers, neighbors, etc.). This makes it difficult for the stigmatized person to resume or continue conventional roles. It tends to place the
person in a milieu of suspicion and social scorn.

A critical issue in labeling theory, then, is how the deviant perceives
what has happened as a result of the public disclosure of his norm-violating
behavior. The juvenile delinquent, for example, may realize that it is no
longer possible for him to maintain a public image of being a "good" person,
since it is now a matter of record at least to social control agencies, that he
is not.

Walter C. Reckless, Simon Dinitz, and Ellen Murray,[50] in 1956, studied
sixth-grade boys in the highest delinquency areas of Columbus, Ohio, who had not
become delinquent and who were not expected to become delinquent, to determine
what insulates a boy against delinquency. A check of police and juvenile court
records was made to confirm the fact that these boys had never been in trouble
with the police. These boys were given a series of four self-administered
scales to complete. These included, in modified form, 1.) the delinquency proneness and 2.) social responsibility scales of the Gough California Personality

Inventory, 3.) an occupational preference instrument, 4.) and one measuring the boy's conception of self, his family, and other interpersonal relations. Also, though not in the presence of the nominee, the mother or mother-surrogate was interviewed with an open-ended schedule to determine the boy's developmental history, pattern's of association, and the family situation. Insulation against delinquency by these boys may be a result of an ongoing process of internalization of non-delinquent values and conformity to the expectations of significant others. Whether the subjects continue to remain "good" will depend on their ability to maintain their present self-images in spite of situational pressures. While this study indicates that a socially acceptable concept of self is an insulator against delinquency, the research does not indicate how the boy in the high delinquency area acquired his self image. It may have been acquired by social definition of role from significant figures (e.g., mother, minister, teacher, etc.), it may be due to effective socialization of the child, or it may be a result of the discovery through experience that playing the part of a "good" boy and remaining a "good" boy bring satisfactions of acceptance to the boy himself. The point is that a positive self-concept seems to be strong enough to insulate the adolescent against delinquency in unfavorable neighborhoods.

Another study, conducted by Walter C. Reckless, Simon Dinitz, and Barbara Kay,[51] was the second phase of a research project on insulation against, and vulnerability to, delinquency at age twelve. Sixth-grade white boys in the highest delinquency areas of Columbus, Ohio, who were nominated by their teachers as likely to come in contact with the police and courts, were compared with boys in the same classes who were previously nominated by the same teachers as most likely to stay clear of contact with the police and courts. The basic instruments consisted of the delinquency vulnerability (DE) and social responsibility (RE) scales of the Gough California Inventory. Also, four items in an occupational preference scale were used in a third instrument which attempted to determine the respondent's self-concept with regard to law abiding behavior, his evaluations of family affectional patterns, his friendship patterns and leisure activities. The evidence supports the initial hypothesis that one's self-concept may be an underlying factor in delinquent or non-delinquent behavior. "Perhaps one of the chief distinctions between persons who will and those who will not experience difficulty with the law in their formative and later years lies in the extent to which a socially acceptable self image has been developed."[52]

There were significant differences in the self-concepts of the "good" boys and the potentially delinquent nominees. The "insulated" boys did not ever expect to be taken to court or jail, attempted to avoid trouble at all costs, rarely engaged in any theft, and had few if any friends who had been in trouble with the law. They liked school, believed they were obedient, evaluated their families as being good or better than most, and felt their parents were neither overly strict or lax. They differed in all of these aspects from those nominated as potentially delinquent. Also, the mothers of the potentially delinquent boys indicated that their sons could have selected better friends, they were often ignorant of their sons' whereabouts, they did not know many of their sons' friends, and the family situation was characterized by conflict. "These differential perceptions on the part of both the boys and their mothers strongly suggest that one of the preconditions of law-abiding or delinquent conduct is to be found in the concept of self and others that one has acquired in his primary group relationships."[53]

Walter C. Reckless and Simon Dinitz[54] studied a group of "good" boys and a group of "bad" boys, as nominated by their sixth-grade teachers in Brooklyn, in 1967. The purpose was to determine whether the trends noted in Columbus applied to the more complex, urban environment of New York. They explored the self-concept as an important self-factor which controls the direction of the person. The authors employed the same research techniques as used in the preceding two studies. There is evidence in the authors' previous research which indicates that the self-concept may be one of the important factors in determining the "drift" toward or away from delinquency and crime. Reckless and Dinitz feel they have found corroborating evidence that the self-concept of the early adolescent may be one of the factors which controls directionality. The teachers' prognostications of sixth-grade boys indicate that directionality, toward or away from delinquent behavior, can be sensed and assessed. The authors believe that these indicators toward or away from deviance point to the strong possibility of a favorable-to-unfavorable self-concept in the young person, which is acting as a controlling agent.

Jack Donald Foster, Simon Dinitz, and Walter C. Reckless[55] studied boys involved in activities definable as crimes under adult statutes in an urban community of 300,000, in 1972. This study examined the extent to which delinquent boys perceive having incurred any social liability as a consequence of public intervention. Cases were gathered consecutively over a period of three months from both the police and the juvenile court simultaneously. All subjects were interviewed within a week to ten days but no more than twenty days after disposition of their cases. A combination of direct and open-ended questions was used by the interviewer. The data indicate that only a very small proportion of the boys interviewed felt seriously handicapped by their encounter with the police or juvenile court. The subjects did not perceive any significant change in interpersonal relationships with family, friends, or teachers. Greatest social liability was perceived in impersonal situations where one's character tends to be inferred from public documents, such as court or police records, rather than through personal acquaintance with the individual. The only social liability perceived by the boys was in the area of contact with the police and future employers. This does not deny the existence of public stigma nor the consequences the delinquent may encounter in future situations. This perception or misperception may be a result of the subjects' inability to project a deviant status into the future. Also, "it is possible that this group of predominantly lower-class boys has accepted and internalized conceptions of limited economic and social opportunities which social stigma would hardly decrease. In other words, the boys may have already neutralized the unfavorable consequences which result from stigma."[56]

In 1964, Michael Schwartz and Sandra S. Tangri[57] asked sixth-grade teachers in an inner-city, all-Negro school in the highest delinquency area of Detroit to nominate "good" and "bad" boys; i.e., to designate which boys they felt would never have police or court contacts and which boys they felt sure would have such contacts. These nominations were checked with police and court records. They sought to determine whether a group of nominated "good" boys and a group of nominated "bad" boys can be distinguished in terms of the quality of self-concept. The phrases to be rated were, "I am," "My friends think I am," "My mother thinks I am," and "My teacher thinks I am." The data indicate that the "bad" boys do have a more negative self-concept than the "good" boys. This supports the notion that two such nominated groups do have different qualities of self-concept.

There are several methological shortcomings in the research on delinquency and self-concept as pointed out by Tangri and Schwartz.[58] First, without a control group of "bad boys," it is impossible to conclude that there is actually a difference in self-concept between the delinquent and non-delinquent populations. Second, court records do not include all cases of law-violating behavior. The non-delinquent group may include boys who were not apprehended or who were not formally processed through the juvenile justice system. Also, the use of teacher's nominations for non-delinquent boys is not infallible. In the Reckless, Dinitz, and Kay[59] study, approximately 11% of the nominations were eliminated because they had already experienced contact with the police or juvenile court. The remaining nominations may result in biased conclusions since they may include a majority of superior students rather than the "average" non-delinquent. Finally, the instruments used to evaluate self-concept must be questioned. Each boy was given the delinquency proneness (DE) and social responsibility (RE) scales of Gough's California Personality Inventory (CPI). "The CPI items obviously are drawn from a middle-class frame of reference, as are the teacher's impressions."[60] It is therefore preferable to use a less culture-bound measure such as the Twenty Statements Test or the Tennessee Self-Concept Test.

Sethard Fisher,[61] in 1972, compared the academic and non-academic grades of two groups of seventh, eighth, and ninth grade students in the Santa Barbara school system. One was a publicly delinquent group, (known by school counselors to be on probation) and the other had no known history of delinquency (confirmed by police and court records). Academic grade averages were based on grades in the major subject, such as English, reading, math, social studies, etc. Non-academic grades were given on such matters as work habits, character, personality factors, etc., based on classroom behavior. The findings suggest that public status as deviant is associated with negative evaluation in conventional situations. But, the data show that the same relationship existed before the experimental group became publicly deviant. "...According to our data, the public label appears not to set in motion a process of differential treatment, rather it appears simply to reflect, and perhaps exacerbate, a process already ongoing."[62]

Therefore, the differences between the two groups may not begin with the label but may have to do with school adaptation prior to the label.

As evidenced by the preceding summary of the previous research concerning self-concept and delinquency, there is little consensus on the effect self-concept has on a youth's behavior. In addition, there has been limited research on the effects of juvenile court proceedings on youth who are labeled delinquent. There is clearly a need for more rigorous research in this area. The intent of this study is to attempt to fill an existing research gap, as well as to test the conceptual scheme developed by labeling proponents and indirectly some tenets of the symbolic interactionist orientation from which much of labeling theory derives. In addition, the study should provide insights which may have practical value when applied to the procedures currently employed in the juvenile justice system.

CHAPTER III

STATEMENT OF PROBLEM AND METHODOLOGY

Specifically, the focus of this study is upon the relationship between juvenile court proceedings and the delinquent youth's self-concept. The way an individual views and interacts with the world around him is partly a function of the way he views himself. His behavior is a reflection or expression of his self-concept, and his self-concept is influenced by his behavior, the reactions he gets from the external world, and his own reactions to himself. There is a constant interaction between his self-concept and his behavior, with each influencing the other. Persons whose behavior is publicly known to be anti-social, delinquent, and criminal should according to the labeling perspective, have deviant self-concepts. This study examines the self-concepts of institutionalized delinquents, delinquents on probation, and a control group of non-delinquents, to determine if a significant difference does, in fact, exist. Theoretically, conceptions of self should be most stigmatized among the institutionalized delinquents, followed by the delinquents on probation, while non-delinquents should possess more positive self-concepts. The study was conducted in a mid-western community with a population of approximately 40,000. An attempt was made to match the age, race, sex, and social class composition of the groups. The sample size for delinquents in the detention facility (Group I) was 29, for delinquents on probation (Group II) was 27, and for non-delinquents (Group III) was 56.

Previous empirical studies indicate that there is some evidence that the delinquent can be differentiated from the non-delinquent on the basis of self-concept. The idea of "commitment shock"[63] holds that the fact of recent arrest, incarceration, and the uncertainty of one's future, tends to cause the young offender to be depressed and to hold more negative self-attitudes than he had prior to commitment, but studies of the effects of differential handling of juvenile cases have been given little attention.

The delinquents studied in the detention center were those who had been sent there by the juvenile court for "rehabilitation." Those awaiting a court hearing or between a hearing and transfer to a correctional school were eliminated from consideration. The center houses approximately fifteen youths at one time and has a program consisting of three stages which each youth must successfully complete prior to his release. Upon completion of each stage, the youth is awarded additional privileges and responsibilities, such as staying up later, home visits, and free time away from the center. Ideally, the program should be completed in three months, but the average length of stay is six months.

Names of youths on probation were obtained from the Director of Court Services in the community to be studied. The child placed on probation remains in the community, usually in his own home. Probation as a disposition usually requires attendance at school, an early curfew, and the avoidance of disreputable companions and places. Although there may be some stigma attached to probation, it is not expected to be as significant as that attached to a child placed in a detention facility.

The control group of non-delinquents consists of youths selected by an accidental sample from the local high school who have not experienced police or juvenile court contact. A check of police and juvenile court records was made to confirm these nominations, and three youths with delinquent records were eliminated from the sample.

Ideally, of course, in order to assess the effects of being adjudicated delinquent upon the self-concept of the juvenile, a before-after with control research design should be employed. That is, some measure of self-concept should be utilized for a group of juveniles none of whom has been adjudicated delinquent. These juveniles would then be re-tested at a later date, when, presumably, some would have been adjudicated delinquent (other important events having been controlled for) and the two sets of data would then be compared. Obviously this would be extremely time consuming, expensive, and probably impossible to accomplish since we seldom have enough control over human subjects to be certain that no other event besides labeling could have caused any observed differences.

The type of design employed in this study is an after only design which makes causal inference very risky. However, the use of a matched control group of juveniles who have not been labeled should enable us to assess the effects of juvenile court adjudication on self-concept, providing no alternative explanation can account for the changes observed. The basic issue to be investigated, then, is whether differences in self-concept exist among the three test groups. If such differences exist, and if no other important event appears to be a feasible cause for such differences, the effects of the labeling process certainly may be considered as a possible causal explanation which may be further investigated in future research.

Clearly the research described here will not allow the researcher to determine whether negative self-concepts cause or result from juvenile court experiences. However, if there are significant differences in self-concept in the predicted direction among the groups, and if self-concepts of delinquents are more negative than those of non-delinquents who differ from the former only to the extent that they have been officially labeled, it would not be unreasonable to suspect that the labeling process contributes to the formation of more negative self-concepts among juveniles.

A study of self-conceptions involves a number of important methodological problems. In the present case, the possibility exists that the non-delinquent sample may include the uncaught delinquent. The absence of a police or court record of delinquency cannot be taken as reliable evidence of the absence of deviant behavior which, if known, would constitute delinquency. For present purposes, then, the absence of an official record of delinquency will be used as an indicator of non-delinquency, but it should be emphasized that this study compares officially labeled delinquents and juveniles who have not been so labeled. Also, police and court intervention does not have an equal effect on all youths, since the type of disposition, previous contact with law enforcement agencies, the nature of the offense, and the amount of public exposure given to the intervention, are important variables. Furthermore, it must not be assumed that a delinquent youth accurately perceives the extent of the liability he has incurred since the extent of the damage may not be immediately visible. Certain types of deviant behavior could be more damaging to some youths than to others, because social liability varies with social positions and situations. Finally a stigma is not stable over time and may be altered by subsequent acceptable or unacceptable definitions. It is extremely difficult to control all of these variables, but an attempt will be made to control the following: type of disposition, previous contact with a law enforcement agency, age, sex, and the nature of the offense. A longitudinal study is suggested to examine the effect time has upon the responses reported in this study.

The primary instrument utilized in this study is the "Twenty-Statements" Test, developed by Manford H. Kuhn and Thomas S. McPartland,[64] which can be found in Appendix A. The device consists of a sheet of paper headed by these instructions:

> "There are twenty numbered blanks on the page below. Please write twenty different answers to the simple question 'who am I?' in the blanks. Just give twenty different answers to this question. Answer as if you were giving the

answers to yourself, not to somebody else. Write the answers
in the order that they occur to you. Do not worry about logic
or 'importance.' Go along fairly fast for time is limited.

The respondents are naive in the sense that they do not receive instruction in the area to which this research is directed. The number of responses per respondent evoked by the instructions may vary from the requested twenty to none.

The responses were dealt with by a form of content analysis. They were categorized dichotomously either as consensual references or subconsensual responses. "These content categories distinguish between statements which refer to groups and classes whose limits and conditions of membership are matters of common knowledge; i.e., consensual; and those which refer to groups, classes, attributes, traits, or any other matters which would require interpretation by the respondent to be precise or to place him relative to other people; i.e., subconsensual."[65] Examples of the consensual category are "student," "girl," "husband," "sociology major," "from Chicago," etc.; that is, statements referring to consensually defined statuses and classes. Examples of the subconsensual variety are "happy," "depressed," "good wife," "too heavy," "intelligent" etc.; that is, statements without positional reference.

Kuhn and McPartland[66] found several interesting features when content was dichotomized. First, from the ordering of responses it was evident that respondents tended to exhaust all the consensual statements they could make before they made any subconsensual ones. Once they began to make subconsensual references they tended to make no more of the consensual variety. This was the case whether a respondent made as many as nineteen consensual references or as few as one.

Second, the number of both consensual and subconsensual references made by respondents varied from twenty to none. The number of consensual and subconsensual statements given by each respondent did not follow in a simple

29

arithmetic relation, such as the number of consensual references plus the number of subconsensual references equals twenty. This was due to the fact that many respondents made fewer than twenty statements. One respondent may make ten consensual statements and no subconsensual while another may make six consensual references, ten subconsensual, and leave four blanks. All consensual statements are placed on one side of the dichotomy, while "no-responses" are combined with subconsensual references on the other. An individual's "locus score" is the number of consensual references made on the test.

These characteristics of the responses satisfy the definition of the Guttman scale. "The scalogram hypothesis is that the items have an order such that, ideally, persons who answer a given question favorably all have higher ranks on the scale than persons who answer the same question unfavorably."[67] "A given question" refers, in this case, to a specific one of the twenty statements, and a "favorable response" refers to a consensual statement--one that places the individual in the social structure.

The items used in a scalogram analysis must have a special cumulative property. The items must be interpreted in terms of content analysis and not in terms of raw responses to the open-ended question. A person who answers the seventh question with a consensual statement has also (in over ninety percent of the cases) made consensual statements to the first six. Since consensuality refers to self-identification, a variable which is numerically cumulative, the criterion of cumulativeness is satisfied in this test. Guttman states, "A third equivalent definition of a scale is the one upon which our practical scalogram analysis procedures are directly based. It requires that each person's responses should be reproducible from the rank alone. A more technical statement of the condition is that each item shall be a simple function of the person's ranks."[68] This is true for the TST. The coefficient of reproducibility for this test is approximately .85.[69] Scores can be assigned which indicate both how many consensual statements are made by each respondent, and which of his responses fall into the consensual category.

The question "who am I?" is expected to elicit statements about one's identity; his social statuses and attributes which he views as relevant. Asking the individual to give these statements "as if to himself" is to obtain general self-attitudes rather than those which may be idiosyncratic to the test situation or those which may be held toward himself in his relation to the test administrator. The request for twenty statements of self-identity recognizes the complex nature of an individual's statuses, questions whether the ordering of responses correlates with the individual's particular position in society, and explores the range of self-attitudes.

Assigning responses to dichotomous categories, consensual and subconsensual references, is based on the self-theory view that the self is an internalization of one's positions in society. Variations in the self-identifications may be due to the variations in the ways individuals in our society have cast their lot within the range of possible reference groups.

The evidence provided by the "Twenty-Statements" Self-Attitudes Test and by its application to known groups has significant theoretical implications. 1.) The consensual references of the self-conception are more salient. Consensual statements are at the top of the hierarchy of self-attitudes. 2.) Persons vary over a wide range in the volume of consensual and subconsensual references in their self-conceptions. People have locus scores which range from zero to twenty. This variable can be correlated with a variety of other attitudes and behavior. 3.) The variation indicated in 1.) and 2.) can be established and measured by empirical techniques of attitude research--the Guttman Scale.

People organize and direct their behavior in terms of their subjectively defined identifications. "These in turn are seen as internalizations of the objective social statuses they occupy, but for prediction we need to have the subjective definitions of identity, in view of the looseness between the social systems and the individual occupants of statuses in them in a society such as ours, characterized by alternatives, change, and collective behavior--in short, a society toward the secular end of the scale."[70] The "Twenty-Statements" Test elicits these self-definitions.

In addition to the open-ended Twenty-Statements Test, a modified version of the Tennessee Self-Concept Test, a structured questionnaire found in Appendix B, and an open-ended interview, found in Appendix C, will be utilized. The Tennessee Self-Concept Test is categorized according to physical self, moral ethical self, personal self (personal self-worth, psychological traits and characteristics), family self (self in relation to the primary social group, family and close friends), and social self (self in relation to the secondary social group). The juveniles are given the opportunity to respond both in their own words and with structured answers. The use of these three instruments should provide more conclusive results than if only one of the instruments was used.

Descriptive statistics, such as percentages, frequency distributions, etc., are used to analyze the data. They are used to describe and summarize a collection of data. No other statistics are utilized since the sample size is small, the samples are non-random, and the research is exploratory in nature.

CHAPTER IV

PRESENTATION AND ANALYSIS OF DATA

The research was conducted in a midwestern community with a population of approximately 40,000. The sample was divided into three groups: juveniles in detention, (Group I), juveniles on probation, (Group II), and non-delinquents, (Group III). Non-delinquents were matched with juveniles on probation and in detention in terms of age, sex, race, and where possible, social class. A check of juvenile court records was made to insure that no one in the non-delinquent group had a record of official delinquency. The following tables indicate the characteristics of the three groups. Percentages of rows, columns, and cells are indicated in parentheses.

TABLE 1

SEX AND DISPOSITION OF JUVENILES

	Disposition	I	II	III	
Sex	Male	18 (62)	26 (96)	44 (79)	88 (79)
	Female	11 (38)	1 (4)	12 (21)	24 (21)
		29 (100)	27 (100)	56 (100)	112 (100)

Table 1 indicates that juvenile males are involved in more juvenile court proceedings than juvenile females. Among the juveniles arrested, 79% (44 of 56) were male, on a ratio of approximately four to one. This coincides with the national juvenile arrest rate. It may be that females are less frequently delinquent than males because of restrictions imposed upon females which curtail their involvement in delinquent activities, or because of the nature of the sex-role socialization they undergo in our society. However, there is also a strong possibility that juvenile authorities are less likely to take formal action against females than males.

TABLE 2

RACE AND DISPOSITION OF JUVENILES

	Disposition	I	II	III	
Race	White	25 (86)	21 (78)	49 (88)	95 (85)
	Black	4 (14)	6 (22)	7 (12)	17 (15)
		29 (100)	27 (100)	56 (100)	112 (100)

Fourteen percent of the juveniles in detention and twenty-two percent on probation are black. Since only approximately 5.2% of the population in this community is black, they are over-represented in the juvenile court system. This may imply that blacks may be more prone toward delinquency, but, it is also conceivable that blacks are stopped more often by the police and dealt with formally more often than whites as a result of race, social class, or area of residence.

Table 3 shows the age and sex distribution for juveniles in detention. The average age for males is 14.77 and for females 15.55. The average age for juveniles in detention in this study is 15.06 years.

TABLE 3

AGE AND SEX DISTRIBUTION OF JUVENILES IN DETENTION

	Age	13	14	15	16	17	
Sex	Male	4 (22)	5 (28)	2 (11)	5 (28)	2 (11)	18 (62)
	Female	0 (0)	1 (9)	4 (36)	5 (46)	1 (9)	11 (38)
		4	6	6	10	3	29

TABLE 4

AGE AND SEX DISTRIBUTION OF JUVENILES ON PROBATION

	Age	13	14	15	16	17	
Sex	Male	2 (8)	8 (31)	7 (27)	2 (8)	7 (27)	26 (96)
	Female	0 (0)	0 (0)	1 (100)	0 (0)	0 (0)	1 (4)
		2	8	8	2	7	27

The average age for the 26 male delinquents on probation is 15.15. The only female on probation is 15 years of age.

Table 5 shows the age and sex distribution of the non-delinquent group. The average age for males is 14.93 and for females, 15.5.

TABLE 5

AGE AND SEX DISTRIBUTION OF NON-DELINQUENTS

	Age	13	14	15	16	17	
Sex	Male	7 (16)	12 (27)	10 (23)	7 (16)	8 (18)	44 (79)
	Female	0 (0)	1 (8)	5 (42)	5 (42)	1 (8)	12 (21)
		7	13	15	12	9	56 (100)

TABLE 6

RELIGION AND DISPOSITION OF JUVENILES

	Disposition	I	II	III	
Religion	Protestant	13 (45)	10 (37)	29 (52)	52 (46)
	Catholic	5 (17)	6 (22)	12 (21)	23 (21)
	None	11 (38)	11 (41)	15 (27)	37 (33)
		29 (100)	27 (100)	56 (100)	112 (100)

Table 6 indicates the types of religious affiliation among the three groups. It was impossible to obtain an exact match with the control group of non-delinquents.

TABLE 7

SOCIAL CLASS AND DISPOSITION OF JUVENILES

	Disposition	I	II	III	
Social Class	Middle	12 (41)	13 (48)	32 (57)	57 (51)
	Lower	17 (59)	14 (52)	24 (43)	55 (49)
		29 (100)	27 (100)	56 (100)	112 (100)

The above table shows that the majority of youth who have come in contact with the juvenile justice system are lower class. Fifty-nine percent of the delinquents in the detention center and fifty-two percent of those on probation are from lower class families. Social class was measured by the perceptions of the director of the detention facility, the probation officer, and teachers for Groups I, II, and III, respectively. In addition, each juvenile was asked to indicate his social class. Due to the fact that Group III contained a majority of middle class juveniles, it was impossible to obtain an exact match for the non-delinquent group in terms of social class.

Table 8 shows that 56% of the white juveniles in detention are from the lower class as opposed to 44% from the middle class. Also, 75% of the blacks in detention are from the lower class, but this sample includes only four blacks.

TABLE 8

RACE AND SOCIAL CLASS OF JUVENILES IN DETENTION

	Social Class	Middle	Lower	
Race	White	11 (44)	14 (56)	25 (100)
	Black	1 (25)	3 (75)	4 (100)
		12 (41)	17 (59)	29 (100)

TABLE 9

RACE AND SOCIAL CLASS OF JUVENILES ON PROBATION

	Social Class	Middle	Lower	
Race	White	12 (57)	9 (43)	21 (100)
	Black	1 (17)	5 (83)	6 (100)
		13 (48)	14 (52)	27 (100)

Table 9 indicates that the majority of white youths on probation are middle class (57%), whereas the majority of black youths on probation (83%) are from the lower class, but again the number of blacks is too small to allow us to draw any conclusions.

TABLE 10

RACE AND SOCIAL CLASS OF NON-DELINQUENT YOUTH

	Social Class	Middle	Lower	
Race	White	31 (63)	18 (37)	59 (100)
	Black	1 (14)	6 (86)	7 (100)
		32 (57)	24 (43)	56 (100)

Table 10 shows that nearly two-thirds of the white non-delinquents are middle class, while the vast majority of black non-delinquents (86%) are lower class. It was partially for the reason that we were not able to match every delinquent with a non-delinquent in terms of social class.

TABLE 11

NATURE OF THE OFFENSE FOR JUVENILE DELINQUENTS

	Nature of Offense	Delinquent Act	Crime	
Disposition	I	10 (34)	19 (66)	29 (100)
	II	3 (11)	24 (89)	27 (100)
		13 (23)	43 (77)	56 (100)

In Table 11, delinquent act refers to an offense for which only a juvenile can be charged. These include truancy, curfew violations, and runaways. The crimes committed by juveniles in the sample include assault, illegal possession of alcohol and marijuana, disorderly conduct, petty larceny, prostitution, robbery, burglary, unlawful possession of firearms, grand larceny, arson and auto theft.

TABLE 12

DISPOSITION OF FIRST OFFENDERS AND RECIDIVISTS

	Number of Offenses	First Offender	Recidivists	
Disposition	I	0 (0)	29 (100)	29 (52)
	II	11 (41)	16 (59)	27 (48)
		11 (20)	45 (80)	56 (100)

All the delinquents in detention are recidivists. Of the delinquents on probation, 59% are previous offenders and 41% are first offenders.

All three groups, delinquents in detention (I), delinquents on probation (II), and non-delinquents (III), were given a modified version of the Tennessee Self Concept Test and the Twenty Statements Test. In addition, the two groups of delinquents were administered an open-ended interview. The Tennessee Self Concept Test consisted of thirty-four questions divided into five categories: physical self, moral-ethical self, personal self, family self, and social self. A copy of the test can be found in Appendix B. The results are given below in terms of frequencies and percentages of favorable responses to each section.

TABLE 13

TOTAL FAVORABLE RESPONSES OF GROUPS I, II, AND III
ON TENNESSEE SELF CONCEPT TEST

Disposition	I	II	III
Physical Self	16 (55)	11 (42)	27 (48)
Moral-Ethical Self	100 (38)	104 (43)	247 (51)
Personal Self	91 (45)	97 (51)	223 (59)
Family Self	166 (48)	162 (50)	372 (57)
Social Self	105 (73)	111 (82)	247 (89)
Combined Totals of Favorable Responses	478 (49)	485 (53)	1116 (61)

Table 13 indicates the non-delinquents have the most favorable overall self-concept, followed by the delinquents on probation, and finally the delinquents in detention. This supports the labeling orientation that the incarcerated individual suffers the most severe stigmatization, with probationers next, with no effect on those who have not been so labeled. This is true for four of the five categories, the exception being physical self. The stereotyped image of the incarcerated delinquent is one of strength and toughness. The majority of

Group I seem to have accepted this.

In the moral-ethical self category, there are several significant differences between the three groups. In response to the question, "I am an honest person," the favorable responses totaled: I (55), II (59), and III (84). The vast majority of Group III, 92%, said they would try to change when they knew they were doing things that were wrong while 80% of Group II and 65% of Group I said they would try to change.

The direction of responses in the personal self category also supports labeling theory. The favorable responses equalled 45% for Group I, 51% for Group II, and 59% for Group III.

Fifty-nine percent of the incarcerated delinquents believe they are "bad" people. They may be accepting the generalized other's definition that "bad" people are those isolated from "good" people in prisons, mental institutions, etc. Thirty-two percent of the probationers believed themselves to be bad, while only fourteen percent of the non-delinquents felt this way. Also, the delinquent group do not believe themselves to be as capable of coping with problems as the non-delinquents. The majority of Group I, 55%, try to run away from their problems, as compared to 44% of Group II, and only 25% of Group III. Nearly two-thirds, 66% of Group I, 44% of Group II, and only 25% of Group III are satisfied with themselves. This response opposes the labeling perspective and suggests a more positive self-concept on the part of the delinquent. Perhaps the juvenile court system, as perceived by the delinquent, has no effect on how he feels about himself. However, type of attitude on the part of the delinquents could be a direct result of labeling. They may feel society will not permit them to achieve future goals and therefore feel forced to be satisfied with themselves as they currently exist. This is supported by responses on the Twenty Statements Test on which approximately 80% of Group III indicated future goals, such as

"I want to go to college," "I want to become an engineer," etc. This type of response was not found on any of the TST's from Groups I and II. In addition, nearly 40% of both Groups I and II indicated during the interview that they felt their chances for employment would be hindered as a result of their contact with the police, thereby forcing them to accept the status society has given them.

In the family self category, 48% of Group I indicated favorable responses, 50% of Group II, and 57% of Group III. Sixty-two percent of Group I and 67% of Group II believed their family is happy, as opposed to 79% of Group III. Among the non-delinquents, 91% feel loved by their family, whereas only 69% and 70% of the juveniles in detention and probationers, respectively, feel loved. In response to the statement, "I feel my family doesn't trust me," 56% of Group I, 52% of Group II, and 25% of Group III agreed. This indicates that the delinquent perceives his significant others perceptions of him as less favorable than the non-delinquent, at least in terms of trust.

In regard to social self, the same pattern exists. Favorable responses totaled 73% for Group I, 82% for Group II, and 89% for Group III. The delinquents have greater difficulty getting along with the secondary social group. In Group III, 89% believed they are cheerful, 82% of Group II, but only 59% of Group I. Nearly 40% of Group I perceive themselves as a hateful person. Only 19% of Group II, and 14% of Group III feel this way. The fact that the incarcerated delinquents are much less cheerful and more hateful may be a result of their social isolation, or of their adopting the stereotyped image of themselves proffered by society. Thus, they may find it harder to relate to others because of the negative self-concept which accompanies labeling.

The overall favorable responses of males, as shown in Table 14, are in the expected direction, with Group I totaling 52%, Group II, 55% and Group III, 62%. Again, Group I has the most favorable responses to physical self. In the family self category, Group II is lowest with 50% as opposed to 54% and 58% for Groups I and III respectively. This may be due to the fact that most probationers are probably living at home and have more opportunities for family conflict than the juveniles in detention.

TABLE 14

FAVORABLE RESPONSES TO THE TENNESSEE SELF CONCEPT TEST
BY SEX AND DISPOSITION - MALES

Disposition	I	II	III
Physical Self	12 (67)	11 (42)	22 (50)
Moral-Ethical Self	60 (37)	104 (43)	192 (49)
Personal Self	62 (50)	97 (51)	184 (61)
Family Self	117 (54)	162 (50)	303 (58)
Social Self	64 (70)	111 (82)	195 (90)
Combined Totals of Favorable Responses	315 (52)	485 (55)	896 (62)

Table 15 compares only female delinquents in detention and female non-delinquents, because the sample of probationers contained only one female. The percentage of favorable responses is higher for Group III in every category.

44

TABLE 15

FAVORABLE RESPONSES TO THE TENNESSEE SELF CONCEPT TEST BY SEX AND DISPOSITION - FEMALES

Disposition	I	III
Physical Self	4 (36)	5 (42)
Moral-Ethical Self	41 (41)	54 (56)
Personal Self	28 (36)	39 (51)
Family Self	44 (33)	65 (50)
Social Self	42 (76)	51 (88)
Combined Totals of Favorable Responses	159 (43)	214 (59)

Tables 14 and 15 indicate that female delinquents have a more negative self-concept than male delinquents. Police and juvenile court contact may be more traumatic for females than for males as the result of societal expectations. The most significant differences between males and females are in personal self (males 50%, females 36%) and family self (males 54%, females 33%). In response to the statement, "I try to run away from my problems," 64% of the girls agreed as opposed to only 45% of the boys. This is supported by the fact that runaways account for 24.7% of girls' offenses but only 5.5% of boys'.[71] Female delinquents do not get along as well with their families as male delinquents. "The common view is that girls get involved in delinquency because of tension-ridden home situations in which they are on poor affectional terms with their parents. This perspective contends that the sexual misbehavior which is common to female offenders represents an attempt on their part to obtain affectional relationships outside the home."[72]

TABLE 16

FAVORABLE RESPONSES TO THE TENNESSEE SELF CONCEPT TEST
BY SOCIAL CLASS AND DISPOSITION - MIDDLE CLASS

Disposition	I	II	III
Physical Self	7 (54)	6 (46)	16 (50)
Moral-Ethical Self	50 (44)	52 (44)	146 (48)
Personal Self	45 (49)	52 (55)	135 (58)
Family Self	82 (54)	77 (55)	221 (55)
Social Self	50 (77)	52 (80)	137 (83)
Combined Totals of Favorable Responses	234 (53)	244 (54)	655 (61)

Table 16 shows that among middle-class juveniles, delinquents in detention have the most negative self-concepts, followed by delinquents on probation, and non-delinquents. This is true for every category except physical self where Group I has the most favorable response.

TABLE 17

FAVORABLE RESPONSES TO THE TENNESSEE SELF CONCEPT TEST
BY SOCIAL CLASS AND DISPOSITION - LOWER CLASS

Disposition	I	II	III
Physical Self	9 (54)	6 (46)	11 (46)
Moral-Ethical Self	50 (35)	57 (45)	102 (46)
Personal Self	47 (42)	44 (43)	88 (50)
Family Self	82 (44)	85 (51)	157 (53)
Social Self	57 (70)	54 (77)	101 (80)
Combined Totals of Favorable Responses	245 (46)	246 (52)	459 (59)

Table 17 also shows that Group I has the least favorable self-concept
in all categories except physical self, followed by Group II, and Group III.
There are no major differences between social class and self-concept as measured
here so it appears the juvenile justice system has an equal effect on each.

Table 18 shows the differences between Groups I and II among juveniles
who committed a criminal offense. The favorable responses are in the predicted
direction in all categories except physical self, where again Group I has the
more favorable response. Due to the samll number of youths who committed

47

juvenile acts, it was impossible to compare these two variables.

TABLE 18

FAVORABLE RESPONSES TO THE TENNESSEE SELF CONCEPT TEST
BY NATURE OF OFFENSE AND DISPOSITION - CRIME

Disposition	I	II
Physical Self	12 (63)	9 (38)
Moral-Ethical Self	68 (34)	91 (42)
Personal Self	65 (49)	87 (52)
Family Self	114 (50)	147 (51)
Social Self	71 (78)	96 (80)
Combined Totals of Favorable Responses	330 (51)	430 (53)

The Twenty Statements Test, found in Appendix A, was the second instrument employed in this study. The number of responses per youth ranged from the twenty requested to zero. The mean was 6.38 for Group I, 9.40 for Group II, and 13.96 for Group III. The responses were dealt with by a form of content analysis. They were dichotomized as either consensual or subconsensual references. Consensual statements refer to groups and classes whose conditions of membership are common knowledge, (male, sixteen years old, student, etc.). Subconsensual statements refer to groups, attributes, or traits that require interpretation by the respondent to place him relative to others, (happy, poor student, bored, etc.). A favorable response refers to a statement with a consensual reference, one that places the individual in a social system.[73] The juveniles in detention averaged the fewest number of consensual or favorable responses, 2.62, followed by probationers, 4.22, and non-delinquents, 5.33. This coincides with the results of the Tennessee Self Concept Test, where it was found that Group I had the least favorable self-concept and Group III the most favorable.

A subjective analysis of the responses of each group shows some interesting differences. The most frequent responses of Group I were, "I am a troublemaker (28), poor student (27), bad person (25), and lazy (22)." The responses were similar for Group II, such as, "I am stupid (30), ashamed (25), confused (24), and weird (21)." The responses tended to be more positive for Group III, where the most common were, "I am smart (31), happy (31), honest (27), and friendly (26)." The responses of the delinquents and non-delinquents differed the most concerning school and future goals. Nearly three-fourths of each delinquent group indicated they are poor students (dumb, stupid), whereas approximately 65% of Group III believed they are good students (intelligent, smart) or average students. One-third of Group III mentioned roles related to school, (member of student council, editor of school newspaper, member of choir, etc.), but none of the delinquents responded in this manner. Also, approximately 50% of the non-delinquents mentioned future goals or career objectives, such as, "I am going to college, going to be a history major, secretary, musician, etc.". None of the delinquents indicated any future plans or desires. The non-delinquents seemed to view school in a more favorable light and were more concerned with their future than the delinquents. The following tables indicate the differences in favorable responses on the TST according to sex, race, and social class.

Table 19 shows that self-concept, as measured by the Twenty Statements

Test, is also in the predicted direction among males and females. Females seem to be more stigmatized than males in Group I, just as we found in the Tennessee Self Concept Test. Group II included only one female, therefore, the results in this area cannot be determined.

TABLE 19

TOTAL CONSENSUAL (FAVORABLE) RESPONSES TO THE TWENTY
STATEMENTS TEST BY SEX AND DISPOSITION

	Disposition	I	II	III
Sex	Male	53 (2.94)	114 (4.38)	239 (5.43)
	Female	23 (2.1)	0 (0)	60 (5.0)
		76 (2.62)	114 (4.22)	299 (5.33)

TABLE 20

TOTAL CONSENSUAL (FAVORABLE) RESPONSES TO THE TWENTY
STATEMENTS TEST BY RACE AND DISPOSITION

	Disposition	I	II	III
Race	White	67 (2.68)	114 (4.38)	272 (5.55)
	Black	9 (2.25)	0 (0)	27 (3.86)
		76 (2.62)	114 (4.22)	299 (5.33)

Table 20 indicates the favorable responses are in the direction predicted by labeling theory. Black responses are lower than white responses in Groups I and III. Group II had only one black so the results cannot be determined in this category.

TABLE 21

TOTAL CONSENSUAL (FAVORABLE) RESPONSES TO THE TWENTY
STATEMENTS TEST BY SOCIAL CLASS AND DISPOSITION

	Disposition	I	II	III
Social Class	Middle	36 (2.77)	73 (5.62)	218 (6.81)
	Lower	40 (2.5)	41 (2.93)	81 (3.38)
		76 (2.62)	114 (4.22)	299 (5.33)

Table 21 shows that the average number of favorable responses is in the predicted direction in both the middle and lower class. In addition, the middle class youths have a more favorable self-concept than lower class youths in each of the three groups.

The final instrument used in this study was the open-ended interview, found in Appendix C. Only 4% of the delinquents perceived any change in interpersonal relationships with family or friends since their contact with the juvenile court system. None anticipated any greater difficulty in school than previously encountered, because they believed the teachers would not know about their trouble or would not care. Approximately one-third of the delinquents expected increased police surveillance as a consequence of their apprehension.

Everyone who felt this way was male, and this included all of the blacks. But, only one individual (from Group I), felt bitter toward the police, while the remainder believed they were only doing their job. All of the juveniles felt the judge and probation officer had been fair with them. Nearly 40% believed their chances for employment would be hindered as a result of their police contact. They felt having a record would be most damaging in this area. Of those who felt they would encounter job discrimination, all were male and all of the black males were included. Approximately one-half of the delinquents believed they could avoid any future trouble with the law, while the remainder hoped they could. This is questionable since all of Group I were recidivists, and 59% of Group II were recidivists. In addition, the majority, 60%, had friends who had been in trouble with the law. The majority of delinquents believed their age at the time of the offense, secrecy of juvenile court records and future good conduct would minimize any negative consequences of their contact with the court system.

The results of this interview indicate, according to the perceptions of the delinquents, that the extent of perceived stigmatization following police or court intervention is over-emphasized in the labeling orientation. Only a very small proportion of the delinquents studied felt they would be hindered by having a record. However, this does not deny the existence of public stigma nor the consequences they may encounter in the future. From interview results, it appears that the delinquents simply do not perceive that their contact with the juvenile court will affect their lives in many ways. This perception or misperception may be a result of their inability to project a negative status into the future. It is also possible that they are unaware that the stigma could grow or become more important with the passage of time, although they do indicate that it could affect them in two ways; increased surveillance by the police and job discrimination.   Finally, it is of course possible that their perceptions about the effects of being labeled delinquent are accurate and that the goals of confidentiality and destigmatization expressed in juvenile court philosophy are being achieved.

CHAPTER V

CONCLUSIONS AND RECOMMENDATIONS

The intent of this study was to determine if differences exist in self-concept among three groups of juveniles in the direction predicted by the symbolic interactionist perspective and labeling theory. In order to accomplish this, two separate instruments, 1.) the Tennessee Self Concept Test, and 2.) the Twenty Statements Test were employed on I.) juvenile delinquents in a detention facility, II.) juvenile delinquents on probation, and III.) non-delinquents, matched in terms of age, sex, race, and in part, social class, who have no official record of delinquency. In addition, Groups I and II were administered an open-ended interview.

The symbolic interactionist perspective and labeling theory lead us to predict that delinquents in detention would have the most negative self-concept, followed by delinquents on probation, and that non-delinquents would have a more positive self-concept if being processed through the juvenile court system is stigmatizing in the manner predicted by our theoretical framework. Results of both the Tennessee Self Concept Test and the Twenty Statements Test were consistently in the predicted direction, while those of the open-ended interview were somewhat ambiguous. The results are discussed below.

One of the primary reasons for the development of a separate court system for juveniles was the avoidance of the stigmatizing court appearance. The juvenile courts made an attempt to minimize this by having informal procedures, closed hearings to the public and press, and limited access to court records. The concern about the negative consequences related to the juvenile court experience is partially a result of the growing interest in labeling theory. Proponents of the societal response perspective attempt to understand the process through which the response to behavior by society creates deviance. The community, or generalized other, defines certain acts as deviant and stigmatizes those who are believed to have committed such acts. The individual may change because of the label and become isolated from the rest of the community. Gradually, the labeled person may begin to behave in a deviant manner as a means of defense or adjustment to the problems created by the societal reaction to his behavior.

If a youth commits a juvenile act or crime and is not apprehended or labeled, he may grow out of his delinquent behavior. But if social control agencies respond to his behavior as "bad," the youth may come to define it and himself as "bad." There is a tendency to define one in terms of his actions. Therefore, a juvenile who is found to have committed an offense is defined a juvenile delinquent by the court. The court appearance may be considered a "status degradation ceremony," where the youth is transformed into a different person.

The results of the Tennessee Self Concept Test and the Twenty Statements Test indicate that the delinquents in detention and probationers view themselves in much the same way that society sees them. The self-concept of Group I is less favorable than that of Group II, and both are less favorable than Group III. They see themselves more as undesirable people, and they do not like or respect themselves as much as the non-delinquents. It may be that the juvenile court serves as concrete evidence of "what kind of person I am." After all, others judge on the basis of such evidence. Why, then, should not the juvenile judge himself on the same evidence? This puts a great deal of the responsibility for the development of an individual's deviant career upon the court system. The actions of social control agencies which are attempting to help a youthful offender may contribute to the development of his deviant identity and to his future deviant behavior. The juvenile court may initiate a vicious circle in which delinquency causes delinquency. However, labeling one as a deviant may have positive effects and result in the deterrence of further deviant behavior. In some instances, labeling may create pressure to bring the deviator back into conformity with group norms.

An important question regarding the juvenile court's role in labeling is whether it initiates or substantiates labels previously applied to youths by family, peers, teachers, etc. Emerson maintains that the court "produces delinquents by validating the prior judgments and demands for action of local institutions encountering problems from troublesome youths."[74] The important labeling experiences for a youth may take place long before he ever comes in contact with the juvenile court. Whether the court creates or legitimates labels, its official decision is a very important aspect. Only the court has the power to permit the community to intervene in a youth's life. This may be the key labeling act of the juvenile justice system.

The fact that one is labeled by a judicial procedure he considers legitimate may have an even greater negative impact on him than if he had perceived it as illegitimate. A label fairly applied is apt to be taken more seriously than one applied in a clearly unfair manner. In this study, all but one of the delinquents felt they had been treated fairly by both the police and the judge. An unfair label is easier to deny. Therefore, one of the worst things we can do, if we are concerned about the effects of labeling, is to develop a court system that both the community and defendants perceive as being fair. Of course a just judicial system is desirable, but it will probably not decrease the negative effects of labeling.

Ninety-six percent of the delinquents in this study felt that the attitude of their parents towards them had not changed as a result of their contact with the court system. This indicates that the parental attitudes toward their children were well set before the court's intervention. However, it is impossible to ascertain whether they regard their children as troublesome and are not surprised they were apprehended by the police, or whether they believe their children are basically good and will turn out well despite their contact with the juvenile court.

A major shortcoming of this study is the lack of a defined time sequence. It is impossible to determine whether a youth's negative self-concept or self-definition as delinquent preceded or followed his initial labeling as a delinquent. Unless his self-conception changed after his first encounter with the law, one cannot attribute the effect to labeling. The delinquency may have resulted from an already existent inadequate self-concept. A longitudinal study by Ageton and Elliott[75] provides some information on this question. They interviewed 2,617 youths in eight California secondary schools, once annually from the ninth through twelfth grades. Self-concept was measured each year by a short form of the Socialization (SO) Scale from the California Psychological Inventory. Data were also obtained from parent interviews, teacher ratings, and school, police, and court records. The results indicate that over a four-year period, white youths who had had police contact showed a significant decrease in self-concept when compared with peers who had no police contact. Neither self-reported delinquency nor the delinquency of one's peer group were as important as police apprehension with regard to explaining a decreasing self-concept. A youth's self-concept was influenced by whether he had been caught by the police rather than by whether he and his friends had ever done anything wrong.

An understanding of the delinquent's self-concept makes his behavior more understandable and a variety of behaviors can be predicted from his self-concept. It is possible that much of the delinquent's negative behavior is a result of the negative views he holds about himself. It is apparent that no permanent changes in one's behavior will be accomplished unless he is also helped to improve his self-image.

There is an interaction effect between self-concept and behavior with each exerting an influence on the other. An individual sees himself as "bad," "inadequate," etc., and acts accordingly. This behavior confirms his own self-concept and the reactions of others also confirm the same image. Also, one's behavior influences his self-perceptions, and that also generates feedback from others.

This interaction concept has important rehabilitation implications. Rehabilitation is concerned with changing individuals. The interaction notion suggests that this might best be accomplished by working on both variables simultaneously, self-concept and behavior. Therefore, effective rehabilitation programs for delinquents should create an atmosphere in which individuals are considered, and helped to believe, that they are of worth and value as people apart from their behavior. However, it is equally important that they be helped to modify and redirect their behavior in order to like and value themselves more and to generate new and different reactions from the generalized other.

It may be surprising to some that most criminals and delinquents have negative self-concepts, that they actually do not like themselves. Often their arrogant and inconsiderate behavior gives the opposite impression. In our society, dominated by middle class morals and values, this type of behavior often creates desires to punish these "bad" persons. They must be convinced they are "bad," "unworthy," "inferior," and made to feel guilty. Actually, in many instances they may already feel this way and their behavior reflects this. Punitive treatment probably serves to reinforce their already negative pattern of living.

We are not suggesting a coddling of criminals approach. Delinquents

58

badly need firm and effective controls, for their own sake as well as society's. However, if they are to be rehabilitated rather than punished, other factors besides control are involved. They should be prevented from engaging in the previous negative behavior and be required to initiate new and positive behaviors so they can begin to generate positive responses from both themselves and others. In order to accomplish this, the treatment or correctional environment must first convey that they are still persons of worth and value despite their previous behavior. Also, it must help the delinquent to avoid negative behavior (control), but more importantly, find new behavior that will be more rewarding. Finally, it must provide the opportunity for rewards for the more positive behavior. Hopefully, the interaction cycle can be reversed to a positive one, where positive self-concept leads to constructive behavior, which results in favorable reactions from both self and others.

The type of design employed in this study is an after-only design which makes causal inference extremely risky. Ideally, in order to assess the effects of being adjudicated delinquent upon the self-concept of the juvenile, a before-after with control research design should be employed. Some measure of self-concept should be utilized for a group of juveniles, none of whom has been adjudicated delinquent. These juveniles would then be re-tested at a later date, when, presumably, some would have been officially labeled delinquent and the data would then be compared. Obviously, this would be too expensive and time consuming for a study of this nature. However, the use of a matched control group of juveniles who have not been officially labeled allowed us, within limits, to assess the effects of juvenile court adjudication on self-concept. The data indicate there are significant differences in self-concept among the three groups in the predicted direction. Clearly, the research described here does not allow the researcher to make causal inferences about whether negative self-concepts are caused by or result from juvenile court experience, but it would not be unreasonable to suspect that the labeling process contributes to the formation of more negative self-concepts among labeled delinquents.

This study raises some interesting questions which require additional investigation. For example, what kind of congruence is there between the youth's perception of changes in family attitude toward him and his family's perception of changes in their attitudes? As the youth goes through the juvenile justice system, what experiences, in addition to the court hearing itself, stand out in his mind as being the most important or most demeaning? In addition to the study of juveniles who continue to reappear in court, we need to study the juveniles who come into court and then manage to stay out of trouble with the law. The labeling perspective opens a rich source of insight and research possibilities along these lines.

FOOTNOTES

1. Haskell, Martin R. and Lewis Yablonski, <u>Crime and Delinquency</u>, Chicago, (1971), p. 274.

2. <u>Ibid.</u>

3. <u>Ibid.</u>, p. 272.

4. "Illinois Juvenile Court Act," section 701-2 and 702-8 in <u>Illinois Criminal Law and Procedure for 1975</u>, St. Paul, West Publishing Company, (1975), pp. 5, 7, 8.

5. Becker, Howard S., <u>Outsiders</u>, New York, (1963), p. 9.

6. Coser, Lewis, <u>Master's of Sociological Thought</u>, New York, (1971), p. 334.

7. Miller, David L., <u>George Herbert Mead--Self, Language and the World</u>, Austin, Texas, (1973), p. 47.

8. Mead, George Herbert, <u>Mind, Self, and Society</u>, Chicago, (1934), p. 155.

9. Miller, <u>op. cit.</u>, p. 53.

10. Glaser, Daniel, <u>Social Deviance</u>, Chicago, (1972), p. 1.

11. Cooley, Charles Horton, <u>Human Nature and the Social Order</u>, New York, (1964), p. 5.

12. <u>Ibid.</u>, p. 182.

13. <u>Ibid.</u>, p. 184.

14. <u>Ibid.</u>

15. Cooley, Charles Horton, <u>Life and the Student</u>, New York, (1927), pp. 200-201.

16. Thomas, William I., <u>The Unadjusted Girl</u>, Boston, (1931), p. 42.

17. <u>Ibid.</u>

18. <u>Ibid.</u>, p. 43.

19. <u>Ibid.</u>, p. 50.

20. Schur, Edwin M., <u>Labeling Deviant Behavior</u>, New York, (1971), p. 8.

21. Blumer, Herbert, "Sociological Implications of the Thought of George Herbert Mead," in Blumer, ed., <u>Symbolic Interactionism</u>, Englewood Cliffs, New Jersey, (1969), p. 65.

22. Schur, <u>op. cit.</u>, p. 8.

23. Lemert, Edward M., _Social Pathology_, New York, (1951), p. 22.

24. _Ibid._, p. 23.

25. Erikson, Kai T., "Notes on the Sociology of Deviance," _Social Problems_ 9, (Spring, 1962), p. 308.

26. _Ibid._

27. _Ibid._, p. 309.

28. _Ibid._, p. 310.

29. _Ibid._, p. 311.

30. Merton, Robert K., _Social Theory and Social Structure_, New York, (1968), pp. 182-183.

31. Erikson, _op. cit._, p. 312.

32. Kitsuse, John I., "Societal Reaction to Deviant Behavior: Problems of Theory and Method," _Social Problems_, 9, (Winter, 1962), p. 247.

33. _Ibid._, p. 250.

34. _Ibid._, p. 253.

35. Becker, Howard S., _Outsiders_, New York, (1963), p. 8.

36. _Ibid._, p. 9.

37. _Ibid._

38. _Ibid._, pp. 12-13.

39. _Ibid._, p. 34.

40. _Ibid._, p. 35.

41. Schur, Edwin M., _Labeling Deviant Behavior_, New York, (1971), p. 24.

42. _Ibid._

43. _Ibid._, p. 41.

44. Goffman, Irving, _Stigma_, Englewood Cliffs, New Jersey, (1963), Ch. 2.

45. Schur, _op. cit._, p. 51.

46. Garfinkel, Harold, "Conditions of Successful Degradation Ceremonies," _American Journal of Sociology_, 61, (March, 1956), pp. 420-424.

47. _Ibid._, pp. 421-422.

48. Ibid., pp. 420-424.

49. From a conversation with Dr. Steven Cox.

50. Reckless, Walter C., Simon Dinitz, and Ellen Murray, "Self Concept as an Insulator Against Delinquency," American Sociological Review, 21, (1956), pp. 744-46.

51. Reckless, Walter C., Simon Dinitz, and Barbara Kay, "The Self Component in Potential Delinquency and Potential Non-Delinquency," American Sociological Review, 22, (1957), pp. 566-570.

52. Ibid., p. 569.

53. Ibid.

54. Reckless, Walter C., and Simon Dinitz, "Pioneering With Self-Concept as a Vulnerability Factor in Delinquency," Journal of Criminal Law, Criminology, and Police Science, 58, No. 4, (1967), pp. 515-23.

55. Foster, Jack Donald, Simon Dinitz, and Walter C. Reckless, "Perceptions of Stigma Following Public Intervention for Delinquent Behavior," Social Problems, (Fall, 1972), pp. 202-209.

56. Ibid., p. 209.

57. Schwartz, Michael and Sandra S. Tangri, "A Note on Self-Concept as an Insulator Against Delinquency," American Sociological Review, 30, No. 6, (December, 1965), pp. 922-26.

58. Tangri, Sandra S. and Michael Schwartz, "Delinquency Research and the Self-Concept Variable," in Juvenile Delinquency, A Book of Readings, by Rose Giallombardo, New York, (1972), pp. 169-180.

59. Reckless, Dinitz, and Kay, op. cit.

60. Tangri and Schwartz, op. cit., p. 173.

61. Fisher, Sethard, "Stigma and Deviant Careers in School," Social Problems, (Summer, 1972), pp. 78-83.

62. Ibid., p. 82.

63. Fitts, William H. and William T. Hamner, The Self Concept and Delinquency, Nashville Mental Health Center, Monograph 1, (July, 1969), p. 25.

64. Kuhn, Manford H. and Thomas S. McPartland, "An Empirical Investigation of Self-Attitudes," American Sociological Review, 19, (February, 1954), pp. 68-76.

65. Ibid., p. 69.

66. Kuhn and McPartland, op. cit.

67. Stouffer, S. A., L. Guttman, E. A. Suchman, P. F. Lazarsfeld, S. A. Star, and J. A. Clausen, _Studies in Social Psychology in World War II: Measurement and Prediction_, Princeton, (1950), p. 9.

68. _Ibid._, p. 62.

69. Kuhn and McPartland, _op. cit._, p. 71.

70. _Ibid._, p. 76.

71. _Ibid._, p. 41.

72. Gibbons, Don C., _Delinquent Behavior_, Prentice-Hall, Englewood Cliffs, New Jersey, (1970), p. 175.

73. Kuhn and McPartland, _op. cit._

74. Emerson, Robert, _Judging Delinquents_, Chicago, Aldine Publishing Company, (1969), p. 275.

75. Ageton, Suzanne, and Delbert S. Elliott, "The Effects of Legal Processing on Self Concept," Boulder: Institute of Behavioral Science, University of Colorado, unpublished paper, (1973).

BIBLIOGRAPHY

Ageton, Suzanne, and Delbert S. Elliot, "The Effects of Legal Processing on Self Concept," Boulder: Institute of Behavioral Science, University of Colorado, unpublished paper, (1973).

Becker, Howard S., Outsiders, New York, Free Press, (1963).

_____, The Other Side, New York, Free Press, (1964).

Blumer, Herbert, "Sociological Implications of the Thought of George Herbert Mead," in Blumer, ed., Symbolic Interactionism, Englewood Cliffs, New Jersey, Prentice-Hall.

Bordua, David J., "Recent Trends: Deviant Behavior and Social Control," The Annals of the American Academy of Political and Social Science, Philadelphia, Vol. 369 (January, 1967), pp. 149-63.

Cavan, Ruth Shonle, Juvenile Delinquency, Philadelphia, J. B. Lippincott, (1969).

Cooley, Charles Horton, Human Nature and the Social Order, New York, Schocken, (1964).

_____, Life and the Student, New York, Alfred A. Knopf, (1927).

_____, Social Organization, New York, Schocken, (1962).

Coser, Lewis A., (ed.), Masters of Sociological Thought, New York, Harcourt Brace Jovanovich, Inc., (1971).

Emerson, Robert, Judging Delinquents, Chicago, Aldine Publishing Company, (1969).

Erickson, Kai T., "Notes on the Sociology of Deviance," Social Problems, 9, (1962), pp. 307-314.

Filstead, William J., (ed.), An Introduction to Deviance, Chicago, Markham, (1973).

Fisher, Sethard, "Stigma and Deviant Careers in School," Social Problems, 20, (Summer, 1972).

Fitts, William H., and William T. Hamner, The Self Concept and Delinquency, Nashville Mental Health Center, Monograph 1, (July, 1969).

Foster, Jack D., Simon Dinitz, and Walter C. Reckless, "Perceptions of Stigma Following Public Intervention for Delinquent Behavior," Social Problems, 20, (Fall, 1972).

Garfinkel, Harold, "Conditions of Successful Degradation Ceremonies," American Journal of Sociology, 61, (1956), pp. 420-24.

Gibbons, Don C., Delinquent Behavior, Prentice-Hall, Englewood Cliffs, New Jersey, (1970).

Glaser, Daniel, Social Deviance, Chicago, Markham Publishing Company, (1972).

Goffman, Irving, "The Moral Career of the Mental Patient," Asylums, Garden City, New York, Doubleday Anchor, (1961).

_____, Stigma, Englewood Cliffs, New Jersey, Prentice-Hall, (1963).

Haskell, Martin R. and Lewis Yablonski, Crime and Delinquency, Chicago, Rand McNally and Company, (1971).

Illinois Criminal Law and Procedure for 1975, "Illinois Juvenile Court Act," St. Paul, West Publishing Company, (1975).

Kitsuse, John I., "Societal Reaction to Deviant Behavior: Problems of Theory and Method," Social Problems, 9, (Winter, 1962), pp. 247-56.

Kuhn, Manford H. and Thomas S. McPartland, "An Empirical Investigation of Self-Attitudes," American Sociological Review, 19, (February, 1954), pp. 68-76.

Lemert, Edwin M., Social Pathology, New York, McGraw Hill, (1951).

Manis, Jerome G., and Bernard N. Meltzer, (ed.), Symbolic Interaction, Boston, Allyn and Bacon, (1967).

Mead, George Herbert, George Herbert Mead on Social Psychology, Chicago, University of Chicago Press, (1956).

_____, Mead, Selected Writing, New York, Bobbs-Merrill Company, Inc., (1964).

_____, Mind, Self, and Society, Chicago, University of Chicago Press, (1934).

_____, Philosophy of the Act, Chicago, University of Chicago Press, (1938).

_____, Philosophy of the Present, LaSalle, Illinois, Open Court Publishing Company, (1959).

Merton, Robert K. and Robert A. Nisbet, Contemporary Social Problems, New York, Harcourt Brace, (1961).

Miller, David L., George Herbert Mead - Self, Language, and the World, Austin, Texas, University of Texas Press, (1973).

Reckless, Walter C. and Simon Dinitz, "Pioneering with Self-Concept as a Vulnerability Factor in Delinquency," Journal of Criminal Law, Criminology, and Police Science, 58, No. 4, (1967), pp. 515-23.

_____, Simon Dinitz, and Ellen Murray, "Self-Concept as an Insulator Against Delinquency," American Sociological Review, 21, (1956), pp. 744-46.

_____, Simon Dinitz, and Barbara Kay, "The Self Component in Potential Delinquency and Potential Non-Delinquency," American Sociological Review, 22, (1967), pp. 566-570.

Scheff, Thomas J., _Being Mentally Ill_, Chicago, Aldine Publishing Company, (1974).

Schur, Edwin M., _Labeling Deviant Behavior_, New York, Harper and Row, (1971).

_____, "Reactions to Deviance: A Critical Assessment," _American Journal of Sociology,_ Vol. 75, No. 3, (November, 1969).

Schwartz, Michael and Sandra S. Tangri, "A Note on Self-Concept as an Insulator Against Delinquency," _American Sociological Review_, 30, No. 6, (December, 1965), pp. 922-26.

_____, "Delinquency Research and the Self-Concept Variable," in _Juvenile Delinquency, A Book of Readings_, by Rose Giallombardo, New York, John Wiley and Sons, Inc., (1972).

Simmons, J. L., _Deviants_, Berkeley, California, Glendessary Press, (1969).

Stouffer, S. A., L. Guttman, E. A. Suchman, P. F. Lazarsfeld, S. A. Star, and J. A. Clausen, _Studies in Social Psychology in World War II, Volume IV: Measurement and Prediction_, Princeton, Princeton University Press, (1950).

Teele, James E., _Juvenile Delinquency,_ Itasca, Illinois, F. E. Peacock Publisher, Inc., (1974).

Thomas, William I., _The Unadjusted Girl_, Boston, Little, Brown and Company, (1931).

Vander Zanden, James W., _Sociology - A Systematic Approach_, New York, Ronald Press, (1970).

APPENDIX A
TWENTY STATEMENTS TEST

There are twenty number blanks on the page below. Please write twenty different answers to the simple question 'who am I?' in the blanks. Just give twenty different answers to this question. Answer as if you were giving the answers to yourself, not to somebody else. Write the answers in the order that they occur to you. Do not worry about logic or importance. Go along fairly fast for time is limited.

1. _____
2. _____
3. _____
4. _____
5. _____
6. _____
7. _____
8. _____
9. _____
10. _____
11. _____
12. _____
13. _____
14. _____
15. _____
16. _____
17. _____
18. _____
19. _____
20. _____

TENNESSEE SELF-CONCEPT TEST

Instructions

The statements in the questionnaire are to help you describe yourself. Please respond to them as if you were describing yourself to yourself. Do not omit any item! Read each statement carefully; then select one of the five responses listed below. On your answer sheet, put a circle around the response you chose.

Responses:	Strongly Agree	Agree	Undecided	Disagree	Strongly Disagree
	1	2	3	4	5

Physical Self

1.	I am an attractive person	1	2	3	4	5

Moral-Ethical Self

2.	I am an honest person	1	2	3	4	5
9.	I do not always tell the truth	1	2	3	4	5
10.	I am a religious person	1	2	3	4	5
17.	I ought to go to church more	1	2	3	4	5
21.	I shouldn't tell so many lies	1	2	3	4	5
25.	I try to change when I know I'm doing things that are wrong	1	2	3	4	5
29.	I do what is right most of the time	1	2	3	4	5
30.	I sometimes use unfair means to get ahead	1	2	3	4	5
31.	I have trouble doing the things that are right	1	2	3	4	5

<u>Personal Self</u> (Self-worth, psychological traits and characteristics)

3. I am a bad person	1	2	3	4	5
5. I am a nobody	1	2	3	4	5
11. I have a lot of self-control	1	2	3	4	5
18. I am satisfied to be just what I am	1	2	3	4	5
22. I am as smart as I want to be	1	2	3	4	5
26. I can always take care of myself in any situation	1	2	3	4	5
32. I try to run away from my problems	1	2	3	4	5

<u>Family Self</u> (Self in relation to primary group, close friends)

6. I have a family that would always help me in any kind of trouble	1	2	3	4	5
7. I am a member of a happy family	1	2	3	4	5
13. I am an important person to my friends and family	1	2	3	4	5
14. I am not loved by my family	1	2	3	4	5
15. I feel that my family doesn't trust me	1	2	3	4	5
19. I am satisfied with my family relationships	1	2	3	4	5
20. I understand my family as well as I should	1	2	3	4	5
23. I treat my parents as well as I should	1	2	3	4	5
24. I should love my family more	1	2	3	4	5
27. I take a real interest in my family	1	2	3	4	5
33. I quarrel with my family	1	2	3	4	5
34. I do not act like my family thinks I should	1	2	3	4	5

<u>Social Self</u> (Self in relation to secondary group)

		1	2	3	4	5
4.	I am a cheerful person	1	2	3	4	5
8.	I am a friendly person	1	2	3	4	5
12.	I am a hateful person	1	2	3	4	5
16.	I am mad at the whole world	1	2	3	4	5
28.	I get along well with other people	1	2	3	4	5

INTERVIEW

1. Since your trouble with the law, do your parents treat you any differently? (teachers, friends?)

2. Do you think getting into trouble with the law will be bad for you in the future? (If so, in what ways?)

3. Have most of your friends been in trouble with the law? (If so, how do you feel about them?)

4. Do you think you will ever end up in jail?

5. Do you think you will stay out of trouble in the future? (If not, why not?)

6. Have you ever been told that you were headed for trouble with the law? (If so, by whom?)

7. How do you feel about the police? (probation officer, judge?)

8. If you found that a friend was leading you into trouble, what would you do?

9. How do you think your friends feel about you since your trouble with the law?

10. What effects has the juvenile court system had on you?